We Made a Song

Doro Globus   Rose Blake

BLOOMSBURY CHILDREN'S BOOKS
Bloomsbury Publishing Plc
50 Bedford Square, London, WC1B 3DP, UK
Bloomsbury Publishing Ireland Limited
29 Earlsfort Terrace, Dublin 2, D02 AY28, Ireland

BLOOMSBURY, BLOOMSBURY CHILDREN'S BOOKS
and the Diana logo are trademarks of Bloomsbury Publishing Plc
First published in the UK in 2026 by Bloomsbury Publishing Plc
Text copyright © Doro Globus, 2026
Illustrations copyright © Rose Blake, 2026
It Takes a Team series devised by Doro Globus

Doro Globus and Rose Blake have asserted their rights under
the Copyright, Designs and Patents Act, 1988, to be identified
as Author and Illustrator of this work

All rights reserved. No part of this publication may be: i) reproduced or transmitted in any form,
electronic or mechanical, including photocopying, recording or by means of any information
storage or retrieval system without prior permission in writing from the publishers; or ii) used or
reproduced in any way for the training, development or operation of artificial intelligence (AI)
technologies, including generative AI technologies. The rights holders expressly reserve this
publication from the text and data mining exception as per Article 4(3) of the Digital Single Market
Directive (EU) 2019/790

A catalogue record for this book is available from the British Library

ISBN: HB: 978-1-5266-7120-2; eBook: 978-1-5266-7511-8;
Audio: 978-1-5266-9375-4

10 9 8 7 6 5 4 3 2 1

Printed and bound in China by Golden Prosperity Printing & Packaging (He Yuan) Co., Ltd., Heyuan City, Guangdong, China

To find out more about our authors and books visit www.bloomsbury.com
and sign up for our newsletters.
For product safety related questions contact productsafety@bloomsbury.com

Please note: this book shows just one of the many wonderful ways a song can
be made. Every musician – and every song – has its own story! The journey
you see here is just one example, and your way might look completely different.
That's the magic of creativity – there's no single right way to make a song. We
hope this book sparks ideas, inspires you to listen closely and maybe even helps
you start creating songs of your own.

To Tristan and Dorothea – D.G.

We Made a Song

Doro Globus · Rose Blake

BLOOMSBURY
CHILDREN'S BOOKS
LONDON OXFORD NEW YORK NEW DELHI SYDNEY

Turn it up! Do you hear that song playing on the radio? It's a song that I was a part of making. Everyone has music inside them — but it takes a team to get it out and into the world.

I want to show you how music-makers get the songs from their hearts into someone else's ears. When a good tune meets a great team, we can have everyone singing.

Songs are short pieces of music that include lyrics – words that might rhyme like a poem and tell a story like a book. They also have a melody or tune, a series of notes that are arranged to make a unique sound that people will want to listen to over and over again.

Songs have a beat and rhythm. These are the parts of the song that hold everything together and make you want to dance! There are all kinds of different styles, or genres, of song.

Most songs have sections: an intro to start, verses to tell different parts of the story, a middle eight (or bridge) that adds contrast and variety, and a chorus. The chorus repeats after each verse to tie it all together – this is what sticks in your head and makes you want to sing along!

So now you know what a song is, let's get started! All songs start with an idea ...

The idea for a song can come from anywhere. It could be a sensation or experience, it could come from talking to family or friends, or it could start with a phrase I read or another song I've listened to.

Once I have some inspiration, I start jotting down ideas for lyrics or playing notes on my piano. I spend days and days like this, trying out different sounds and combinations of words.

I play my melody and try out different lyrics over and over, recording and playing everything back, and then changing and adjusting it all until ... it hits me!

But that's just the start! The song doesn't really take shape until other musicians get involved. Let's meet the band!

Bassist

"I work with the drummer to keep the song's rhythm steady. My bass guitar has four strings, a long neck and plays very low notes."

Drummer

"My drum kit has lots of parts! The snare and bass drum keep the beat, the tom drums add flair between sections and the cymbals (two big ones and a hi-hat) make explosive sounds. My drumsticks are dented from drumming so hard!"

Lead singer

"I step on stage and speak directly to the audience about the music, the mood, the energy. My voice and the microphone are my instruments. I sing my heart out and love dancing in front of a crowd."

Guitarist

"I help lead the melody, play the chorus and add solos. My guitar is played by strumming, plucking and tapping the strings along the frets."

Keyboardist

"My electronic keyboard creates all sorts of sounds. It can play like a piano, or sound like drums or even a trumpet! It also makes fun effects and noises you can't make with normal instruments. I love experimenting with these sounds."

I play the band my idea. I can tell they like it, because they pick up their instruments and start playing along. This is when the magic really starts to happen!

For this song, the band works together to develop the chord progression, which is a sequence of chords (groups of notes played together) that follow each other in a way that sounds great. We also decide on the rhythm, vocal harmonies and how the song starts and finishes. The ending needs to be a great moment that our listeners won't forget!

Everything needs to work together, so we have to practise to get it right. Then we make a demo (a rough recording of our song). Now it's time to share it with more people!

When we feel ready to rock, we invite our manager to listen to our demo. She's like our super boss and is in charge of everything – from helping us become stars and making sure we get paid, to handling complicated conversations and having our backs when things get hard.

Manager

"I share my ideas and come up with a plan to get the song heard by record labels. It can take a lot of time and lots of calls and emails to find a label that can make the band's dreams a reality."

Great news! Our manager shared our demo and got us a record deal. Now, we need to work with the right producer who will help us shape our song.

Music producer

"I work with the band in the recording studio. I suggest changes, help choose what to keep or cut and help them give their best performance. I also work alongside the recording engineer, who sets up the studio equipment to capture the sounds."

To record our song properly, we head to the recording studio. We can't wait to hone our sound into something special!

The big moment is here! At the recording studio, our producer introduces us to everyone who works there, including our recording engineer. It's their job to get everything ready. They set up the microphones, and make sure the instruments (and the team) are prepared and the equipment is working. Shall we take a look around?

Studio technician
"I maintain all the technical equipment, check the cables are plugged in properly, ensure there's no unwanted sounds and, most importantly, that everything turns on!"

Assistant engineer
"I work at the digital audio workstation – refining, tidying up and editing the recorded sound as it comes in so it's ready for the mixing engineer."

Intern
"From getting tea and coffee to picking up new guitar strings, I am here to help and learn – doing whatever I can to support everyone. It is so exciting to be around the band!"

Instrument technician
"I make sure all the instruments are properly tuned and fix anything that's not working or broken, like a snapped guitar string."

The band
"In the live room, we start recording some elements, like the backing vocals and background sounds. When we need to get the main vocals down, we will move into a smaller, sound-absorbent booth."

Recording engineer
"Following the music producer's lead, I record all the instruments and vocals, making sure there are no unwanted sounds mixed in. I want the musicians to sound their best and help make the song amazing."

Session musician
"I'm not in the band, but they have invited me as a special guest musician to add something different to their song."

It takes days in the studio to get our song right. We record over and over again – sometimes together and sometimes on our own. Usually, the drums and bass will be first. This part is called the 'bed' because it sets the feel and speed of the song. It is also what all the other elements of the song rest on. Then we add guitars, keyboards and other instruments. The singing usually comes last.

Each type of sound is recorded separately through microphones on different 'channels', which become separate 'tracks' in the recording software. I like to imagine each track as its own distinct 'voice', can you imagine listening to each track of a song on its own?

Once the producer is happy, all the sounds that have been carefully captured by the recording engineer get sent to a mixing engineer who blends them together to create a nearly finished version of our song. This is called the 'final mix'. It is always so exciting to hear what the mixing engineer does when they bring all the parts together.

Mixing engineer
"My job is to mix all the recorded sounds (like vocals, drums and guitars) to create a brilliant final mix of the song. I use special equipment, including a mixing desk with lots of knobs and buttons to adjust levels, tones, effects and more, helping everything fit together perfectly."

Once the band and producer approve the final mix of the song, the mastering engineer (known for having the best ears in the business) adds the finishing touches. They're the last person to work on the song, giving it a final polish to ensure it sounds great wherever it's played.

Mastering engineer
"I make sure everything sounds just right for your ears, whether you're listening on the radio, a record player, a phone or through your speakers."

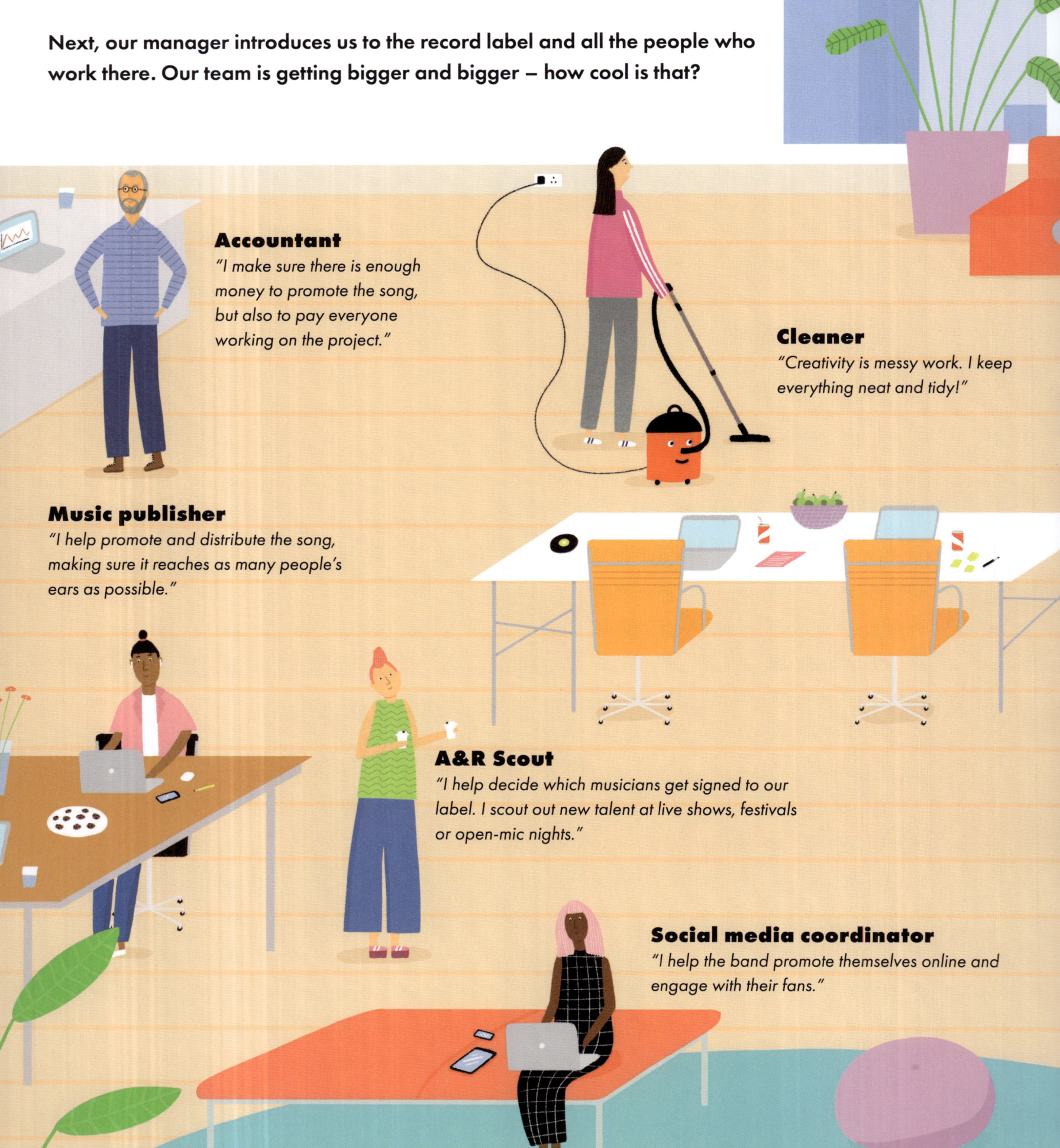

Radio plugger
"I share the song with radio stations and DJs to get it played as much as possible."

Publicist
"I set up interviews for the radio, TV, magazines and newspapers."

Stylist
"I help dress the band, creating a look that is sure to make them stand out!"

Marketing manager
"I work to coordinate how the song is promoted through advertising, emails, concerts and more!"

Booking agent
"I work to book concerts and tours for the band all over the world."

Everyone at the label works with us to get the song ready to bring into the world. Together, we make a plan about how to share it as far and wide as possible. Our song will really come alive when our audience can sing along!

Before we get too excited – there's more work to do. It's time to think about the whole package! First, it's back to the recording studio where we turn our one song into collection of multiple songs. This is called an album.

Once the album is ready, we hire an artist and designer to create the album cover and other materials to share online, in shops and at concerts.

Graphic designer
"I'm trusted to create something special for the look of the album. I listen to the music over and over, using notes from the band to guide me. It's all about capturing the right vibe, so we can portray the music properly on the cover, posters, T-shirts and more."

We also work with a photographer to capture our look and vibe. Whether it's during a photo shoot or while we are onstage, they document everything from us jamming out in front of a crowd to the quiet moments behind the scenes.

These photographs are used in the liner notes for our album, on our website, social media and more. The way we represent our sound visually is really important to us. It's often the first contact the audience has with our music — and we want you to love it!

There's another really important step in getting our sound seen — and that's through making our very own music video!

Director
"I oversee the whole process of making the video — from the filming and editing, to the casting and lighting decisions."

Choreographer
"I create and direct the dance routine for the music video and concerts. The movements echo the songs and add another element to the music."

We work with a creative team to come up with a concept and get to work. It's a complicated process involving loads of talented people – directors, producers, camera and lighting operators and more. It's hard work, but a great way to tell the story of our song!

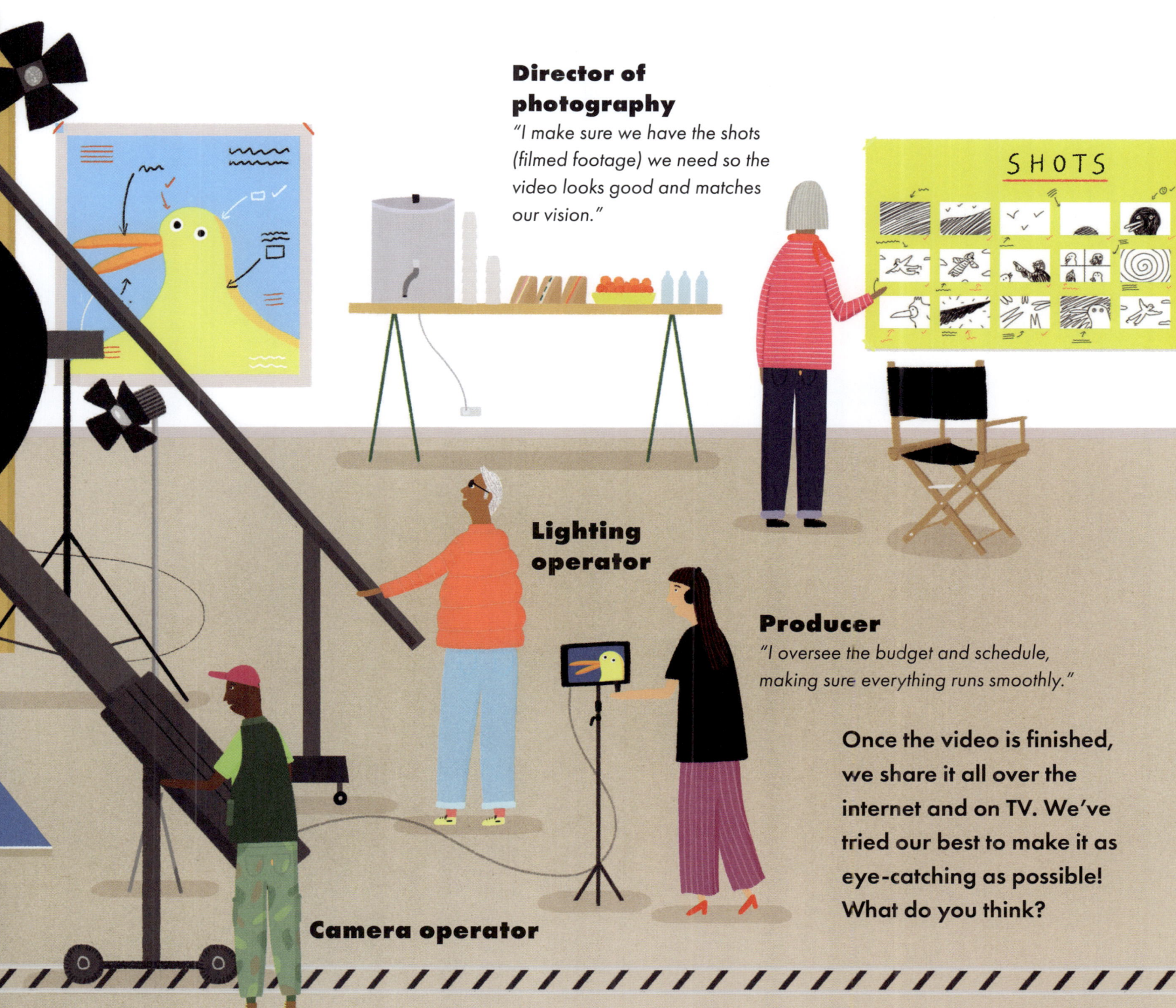

Director of photography
"I make sure we have the shots (filmed footage) we need so the video looks good and matches our vision."

Lighting operator

Producer
"I oversee the budget and schedule, making sure everything runs smoothly."

Camera operator

Once the video is finished, we share it all over the internet and on TV. We've tried our best to make it as eye-catching as possible! What do you think?

Turn up the volume! Can you hear what's playing?

After a lot of hard work and the help of many, we are ready to release the song and hopefully get people dancing! Our label has secured deals with streaming platforms and radio stations, spreading the buzz so our song can be heard everywhere – from a local café to your bedroom.

If the song catches on, we might be invited to play our song on a talk show or be interviewed for a magazine. But really, it's even more exciting when we see a fan wearing our T-shirt or copying our hairstyle. We want as many people as possible to find joy in our creation.

With all the buzz around our new song, we hit the road and go on tour! We can't wait to perform for our fans. We travel from city to city all over the world and often have no real break between different shows. It's tiring but fun work, and we couldn't do it all without our amazing road crew.

Security team
"We make sure that the members of the band are kept safe and that no one comes backstage without permission."

Roadies
"We keep everything running behind the scenes. We set up, take down and manage sound, lighting and stage equipment – making sure everything is working and accounted for before, during and after the performance. The band rely on us to keep the show on the road!"

Merchandise crew
"We sell t-shirts, hoodies, stickers, badges, hats and more – all with the band's designs on them. This is an important part of how we connect with fans and earn money to pay for the tour."

Live sound engineer

"I tour with the band and make sure that the sound quality for the musicians and the audience is always amazing – no matter where we are or whatever sound system we use."

Lighting designer

"I manage the stage lighting. With my lighting crew, I also use visual effects to enhance the mood of the show and make different parts of the song stand out. Sometimes, we even use pyrotechnics (fireworks)!"

Tour manager

"I make sure the band are getting to gigs on time and solve any problems we might have, from issues with stage set-up to last-minute travel disruptions. It's a big job – a concert tour might have up to 50 stops around the world!"

The rush of hearing an audience sing along while we play our song makes my hairs stand on end – it's electric! Just a little while ago the song only existed as an idea in my head ... and now it's in the air all around us.

I might have had the first idea, but it took a talented team to make our song sing. From musicians and engineers to designers and roadies, every part matters. So, next time you hear your favourite song, remember — it didn't take just one person, but a whole team like ours working together to bring the music to your ears.

Let's hear it for our top team!

And want to know the best part? You could be part of this magic too! Whether you love writing, singing, filming, dancing, designing or mixing sounds, there's a place for everyone in the world of music. Let's make some noise!

Ask an expert

Interview with Eric Krasno
Two-time Grammy-winning guitarist, musician and producer

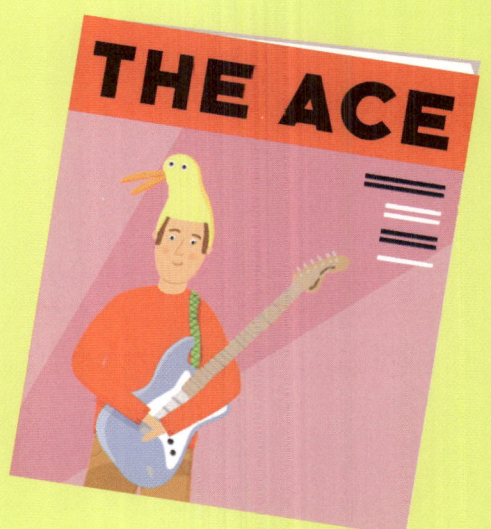

What is your job?
I'm a songwriter, guitarist and producer – but play a part in many aspects of the music-making process. As a producer, I guide the artist's vision, choose material for the songs, pick engineers to work with, help shape the overall sound and support the creative process. Sometimes I'll also play the instruments, act as engineer and sing backing vocals. I'm there to fill whatever role is needed to keep things moving.

What's your favourite thing about working in the music industry?
Seeing how our music impacts people! Watching their joy, and feeling it myself when I listen to something I've worked on, is incredible. Whether I'm onstage or not, seeing an audience sing or dance to a song I helped create is such a cool experience. It's one of the most unique and fulfilling parts of making music.

Did you always know you wanted to work in music? How did you end up doing it?
I was obsessed with music as a kid – always digging through my dad's records and dreaming of being in a band. Violin and piano lessons didn't stick, but everything changed when I got a guitar and heard Led Zeppelin. My brother's band practised in our basement, and that just lit a fire in me! Later, I started my own band, hustled for gigs, put up flyers, rehearsed non-stop and kept writing. When we got signed to a major label, I soaked up everything! It was amazing learning from all these big producers and engineers.

Why do you think teamwork is important for making music?
Teamwork is everything! I have to remind myself that just because you *can* make a lot of music yourself with modern technology, doesn't mean you always *should*! I believe the best music is made with a group – and it always has been. Playing off of one another is what makes the

music the best it can be. I've always enjoyed looking through album covers to see who did what. These days, engineers and others behind the scenes don't always get credited properly— even though they're such a vital part of the process. The music wouldn't be the same without them!

Has anything really funny ever happened to you in your job?

We've had a lot of bus and van breakdowns over the years, where we thought we might miss the gig. We once toured with the Rolling Stones and at the first show, the car never showed up! We ended up in a beat-up old taxi with our gear tied in a wooden box with a bungee cord. When we rolled up, the security guard looked at us and said, "There's no way *you're* the band". Luckily, they let us in once we convinced them!

Do you have to be really good at singing or playing an instrument to work in music?

Definitely not. For example, an engineer's job is mostly about understanding the equipment, and a manager's role is all about communication, organisation and supporting artists. There are lots of jobs in music that don't require you to be a performer. That said, a lot of those roles are still filled by people who've spent their lives soaking up music — listening to it, playing it, learning how it works — because they genuinely love it.

You don't need to be a musician, but you do need that passion. It's a tough industry, so loving music really helps. And if you do? That's what makes it all worth it.

What advice would you give someone who loves music and dreams of working in it one day?

The best advice I can give is: do what you love, every day. If you love music, keep listening, keep exploring and keep making it in whatever way you can. The best music always comes from people who truly enjoy what they're doing — you can hear the joy in it. You don't have to be the most famous or the flashiest person in the room to be part of something amazing. If you find a place in music that makes you happy, then you've already won. That passion is what carries you forwards.

Write your own song

Maybe our song has inspired you to write your own? Why not give it a go yourself – or join a team and create something together? Try, create, discover and learn with your own top team!

Here are my top tips for writing a song:

1. Start with the music

Find a tune with no lyrics – or make your own! How does it make you feel? Let the mood inspire your song.

2. Feel the beat

Clap or tap along to the rhythm. How many beats are there in a line? Use the beat to help shape the flow of your lyrics.

3. Pick your topic

What do you want your song to be about? Adventure? Friendship? Love? School? Jot down words, feelings or stories that come to mind.

4. Write your lyrics

Turn your ideas into words that fit the rhythm of your tune. Use playful language like similes or metaphors to bring your words to life!

5. Perform it!

Say or sing your lyrics out loud. Do they match the music? When you're ready – share your song. You could even record it or put on a performance for your friends and family!

Glossary

A&R (Artists & Repertoire) the department of a record label responsible for finding new talent

album a collection of recorded songs on a CD, record or other digital format

chord when two or more notes are played at the same time to create a sound known as a 'harmony'

chord progression a sequence of chords played one after the other to create the harmony of a song

demo a rough or sample version of a song, short for 'demonstration'

DJ (disc jockey) someone who plays recorded music for an audience, usually on the radio or at a club

fret a thin, metal strip on the neck of a stringed instrument (like a guitar) where musicians place their fingers on the strings to play different notes

hi-hat a pair of cymbals on a stand, played with a foot pedal or drumsticks, used to keep rhythm in a drum kit

liner notes written information about the music or performers that comes with a CD or vinyl record

live room the main space in a recording studio where musicians perform and have their music captured by microphones

merchandise products that are associated with a musical artist or band, like T-shirts, mugs or bird-shaped hats

middle eight sometimes called a bridge, section of a song which is usually (but not always) eight bars long and adds some contrast or variety to the song

pitch how high or low a sound is

record label a company that works with an artist or band to record and sell their music

recording studio a place specially designed to record, mix and produce music

solo a song, or part of a song, which is performed by just one singer or musician

sound-absorbent booth a room specially designed to block any outside noise

streaming platforms online services which broadcast videos or music over the internet

tempo the measure of how fast or slow a piece of music is, which is measured in BPM (beats per minute)

vocals sounds created by the human voice

Author's note

This series is dedicated to my children Tristan and Dorothea, whose curiosity and creativity fuels my own.

Thank you to Rose Blake for helping me shape the series and for the love you poured into this book. A special thank you to my dear friends Eric Herman and Andrew Aprile, whose love for music and expertise in the field was a huge help in the process. Thank you to Leo Clarke, Lawrence King and Chris Johnson for consulting on this project, and to Eric Krasno for sharing his experiences in our interview.

Thank you to the talented team at Bloomsbury: Lara Hancock for seeing the potential in the series, my editor, Emily Ball, for her dedication and teamwork and to Katie Knutton for the wonderful design. Thank you also to Céline Culliford, Barney Duly, Sophie Harrington and everyone in rights, sales, marketing, publicity and production. I am grateful to all of the publishers who have taken the series, to the booksellers and educators around the world and to my wonderful agent James Spackman who helps make it all possible.

Last but not least, thank you to my family: my parents and brother who cheer me on (always), my children, nieces and nephews who review my projects, and my husband who helps create the space for me to work on these books.

Thank you to you, the readers, for choosing this book.

It really does take a team!

Doro

About the creators

Doro Globus is a writer, editor, and publisher who loves sharing stories about art, creativity and how things are made. As publisher at David Zwirner Books, she has spent over 15 years working with artists and writers around the world. Passionate about helping children (and adults!) discover the creative work behind everyday things, Doro hopes to make these worlds more open and accessible. She was born in New York and now lives in London with her husband and two children.

Rose Blake is an artist and illustrator based in London. She has illustrated several acclaimed children's books, including *A History of Pictures for Children*, which won the New Horizons Award at the Bologna Children's Book Fair. Rose loves finding playful, thoughtful ways to tell stories through images and continues to bring curiosity, humour and imagination to everything she makes.